T0033479

Pitch Perfect and Persistent!

The Musical Debut of Amy Cheney Beach

" . . . no other life than that of a musician could ever have been possible for me. "

Caitlin DeLems   Illustrated by Alison Jay

CALKINS CREEK

AN IMPRINT OF ASTRA BOOKS FOR YOUNG READERS

New York

Amy Cheney toddled around the Henniker, New Hampshire, farmhouse and hummed a tune. One after another. Forty pitch-perfect songs— precisely in the key she had first heard them.

Music-making filled Amy's home.

The Cheney family didn't have luxuries, but they did have a clarinet and Mamma's piano. Clara Cheney taught music lessons and could play the piano with her eyes closed. She also sang soprano in the church choir and warbled some more while scrubbing at the washboard.

Amy ALWAYS lent an ear.

Charles Cheney labored long hours at Grandpa's paper mill.
When Papa returned home, he tapped his work-worn boots—
but never in time to Mamma's music.

And Amy kept right on listening.

In 1868, one-year-old Amy demanded songs. She knew what music she wanted to hear. When she wanted to hear it. And how she wanted it sung.

At two, Amy belted out an anthem from start to finish. No mistakes.

Friends and relatives marveled. Mamma worried.

Amy MUST grow up as a *normal* child. Not a musical prodigy!

Mamma stuck by her strong religious beliefs.

No indulgence. No spectacle. And certainly, no piano!

But Amy's love for music only grew.

Mamma clung to her conviction. NO PIANO!
Stubborn. Steadfast. Amy tried to sit on Mamma's lap to
reach the black and white keys. NO PIANO!
She climbed on a stool.
NO PIANO!
Amy implored. Coaxed. Whined.

But no one could stop Amy from HEARING music.

No one could stop her from THINKING music.

No one could stop her from PLAYING music—*her* way.

While her fingers struck her imaginary keyboard, Amy burst into songs—
including her own melodies to Mother Goose rhymes.

She stored every note, every measure, to memory.

Mamma continued to fret. Amy continued to shock, shake, and boggle the minds of those who met her.

Amy linked the key of music to a color and mood. "Play the pink or blue music," she demanded. Mamma obliged. Happy, light music in the key of E-flat major (pink) or A-flat major (blue) filled the room. But when Mamma played in a minor key—swirling in its dark moods—Amy covered her ears and cried.

Even though Amy taught herself to read at three, even though she understood music, the piano still remained off-limits . . .

. . . until Aunt Franc, Mamma's only sister, arrived from California.
She plopped four-year-old Amy on the piano bench.

Baffled, Mamma objected. Aunt Franc persisted. And Amy pounced
into action.

REAL piano keys! Cool. Smooth. Alive.

Musical ideas locked inside her escaped. A waltz floated out. Harmonies
joined simple melodies.

Music fired inside her like a Fourth of July cannon cracker.

Amy composed three waltzes—all in her head.

She passed a perfect-pitch test—child's play. Transposed music—effortless.
Recited L-O-N-G poems—a snap.

"At last, I was allowed to touch the piano . . . I played at once the melodies I had been collecting, playing in my head, adding full harmonies to the simple, treble melodies."

At six, she launched into piano lessons. Academic lessons. All in the home parlor, all under Mamma's instruction.

A year later, Amy pounded out Bach, Mozart, and Mendelssohn. Handel and Chopin. Beethoven soon captured her attention.

Headstrong, Amy pleaded and negotiated.
She wanted in the worst way to perform.
Finally, Mamma relented.

At her first recital, Amy performed a Chopin waltz and her *own* waltz.
At her second, a musicale, she added a Beethoven sonata. Two Boston
concert managers offered contracts. Amy's parents flatly refused.
No more recitals—even at private events.

NONE!

Eight-year-old Amy's family moved to Boston, the hub of classical music, home to famous composers and performers and first-rate concerts. Opportunities unfolded like notes on a music score.

Amy didn't want to miss out!

She begged and bargained—and Mamma softened.

Amy's new piano instructor soon arrived.

Papa and Mamma enrolled twelve-year-old Amy in one of Boston's top-notch schools—a REAL school. Fascinated by mathematics, science, and foreign languages, Amy excelled. Her skills skyrocketed.

And Amy continued to play the piano.

She practiced FOUR long hours every day!

Amy's music teachers agreed she was the greatest musical prodigy of America. Celebrated musicians encouraged her debut.

Not Amy's parents.

Society did not approve of middle-class girls and stage careers. Marriage—marvelous. A piano teacher—perhaps. A *serious* musician—certainly not!

But Amy WAS serious!

Finally, Mamma made a MONUMENTAL decision.

Convinced a piano debut would help secure a future husband for fifteen-year-old Amy, Mamma grudgingly consented.

Amy's music course changed as quickly as a staccato note.

One month after her sixteenth birthday, Amy stepped out of the wind-driven
rain and into Boston Music Hall!

She walked across the stage and sat at the piano. Her posture ramrod straight.
Two long and heavy golden plaits hung neatly down her back.

The conductor cued. The orchestra began.

Amy's fingers lit upon the ivory keys. Her small hands leapfrogged, passing in a blur.

Up the keyboard. Down the keyboard.

With not an ounce of stage fright, she performed two major works—Moscheles's Concerto in G Minor, Chopin's Rondo in E-flat Major.

ALL from memory.

The audience was "enthusiastic in the extreme." Flowers were wildly "heaped upon her." The critics did not hold back in their reviews. Nine Boston papers and the *New York Tribune* all concluded Amy Cheney was a SMASHING hit!

"I can only compare my sensations with those of a driver, who holds in his hands the reins that perfectly control a glorious, spirited pair of horses. One must live through such an experience to properly appreciate it."

Amy kept on going. Could not stop! Would not stop!

She published her first composition. Prepared for her next public recital—only three months away.

Amy Cheney was out in the world. Everyone could hear her now!

"Life was beginning!"

THE RAINY DAY
Longfellow
Amy Marcy Cheney

With Violets

"If you feel deeply and know how to express what you feel, you make others feel."

AUTHOR'S NOTE

In Amy Cheney Beach's lifetime, America's women battled for equal rights. The nineteenth century witnessed Susan B. Anthony, Elizabeth Cady Stanton, and Lucy Stone lead the suffrage movement; Belva Lockwood run for president; and Elizabeth Blackwell break barriers in the medical field. The early twentieth century saw aviators Ruth Law and Amelia Earhart spark headlines.

On January 9, 1884, three months after her sensational debut, sixteen-year-old Amy Cheney gave her next public recital to a packed Chickering Hall in Boston. The critics agreed that her performance "justified fully all the expectations." Afterward, Amy went on the road performing, her mother always nearby.

At seventeen, Amy Cheney desperately wanted formal training in composition. But society believed women were less intelligent, less able to learn. Boston's ranking music conductor, Wilhelm Gericke, recommended she teach herself. Headstrong, Amy took Gericke's advice. She analyzed the music scores of great masters and pored over composition and music theory manuals.

Between 1883 and 1885, she made her way to concert halls in Boston, New Hampshire, and throughout New England. There she performed with leading orchestras, as well as America's most renowned conductor, Theodore Thomas.

Amy Cheney won over many Boston hearts, including widower Dr. Henry Harris Aubrey Beach. In 1885, at eighteen, she married the forty-two-year-old surgeon. Along with her vows, she honored an arrangement to limit a performance career on stage for a career of composing. "I was happy and he was content," she wrote. Henry *allowed*, and Amy agreed to, one public recital a year, in addition to several performances for charity.

Known as Mrs. H. H. A. Beach, both privately and professionally,

she now focused on composing full-time and continued to publish. "It was [Henry] more than any one else who encouraged my interest upon the field of musical composition in the larger forms," she wrote. "It was pioneer work, at least for this country, for a woman to do . . ."

Several months after their marriage she took on a bold project, composing the Mass in E-flat (an hour and a half in length) for solo voices, chorus, organ, and orchestra. Six years later, in 1892, the premiere of her completed mass was greeted with surprise and admiration. "Waving of handkerchiefs and clapping of hands"— and the stomping of feet—echoed throughout the concert hall. Amy Beach became the first American woman to receive widespread fame as a composer of a large-scale work for orchestra.

The next year, at a dedication of the Woman's Building at the World's Columbian Exposition in Chicago, she triumphed with her *Festival Jubilate*, op. 17. Three years later, at twenty-nine, she stepped out with her *Gaelic* Symphony (Symphony in E Minor, op. 32), premiered by the Boston Symphony Orchestra. *Gaelic* was a landmark success. Beach became the first American woman to write a symphony premiered by a leading American orchestra!

The *Gaelic* Symphony borrowed several Irish folk songs as themes, and in her later works she often drew from folk music of various cultures. Future performances were given by major orchestras in cities across the country from New York to San Francisco—even Europe.

In June 1910, her husband died, followed seven months later by her mother. On September 5, 1911, her forty-fourth birthday, Amy Beach sailed to Europe for the first time. She promoted her music, secured a concert manager, reestablished herself as a concert artist—and received glowing reviews. With the outbreak of World War I in 1914, she returned to the United States where she continued to give concerts.

Starting in 1921, she spent warmer seasons at the MacDowell Colony in Peterborough, New Hampshire, an artists' colony where she composed among nature and bird songs. The MacDowell

Amy Beach (center) and other women composers attend a convention for the National League of American Pen Women in Washington, DC, April 23, 1924. The League, founded in 1897, was made up of professional women in letters, arts, and music.

Colony provided a place of quietude and daily contact with other musicians and young artists whom she encouraged and supported.

She also frequented "The Pines," her summer home in Centerville, MA, on Cape Cod, where she enjoyed "heavenly" time "luxuriating in the daily 'swim.'" During colder seasons, she divided her time between concerts and her New York apartment. She desired the country for creative stimulation and the city for cultural fulfillment.

Amy Beach continued to bring her work to the stage across America and Europe. Twice, she visited and played for First Lady Eleanor Roosevelt at the White House. At one event, in 1934, four hundred guests gathered in the East Room of the White House to celebrate Beach's "Golden Jubilee," the fiftieth anniversary of her musical debut.

In 1940, Amy Beach gave her last performance, her Piano Trio, op. 150, in Brooklyn, New York. Two years later, a festival held at the Phillips Gallery in Washington, DC, honored her seventy-fifth birthday. Over the two-day event, all of her chamber works were performed.

On December 27, 1944, Amy Beach died from heart disease at the age of seventy-seven in her New York apartment, a devoted friend at her bedside. New York's St. Bartholomew's Episcopal Church, still adorned with Christmas poinsettias and featuring a full choir, held funeral services. She was laid to rest in Boston's Forest Hills Cemetery next to her husband and parents.

Amy Beach published over three hundred works. At a time when women were establishing roles in many professions, she helped bring female musicians out of the piano parlor, onto the stage, and into the music publishing world.

Amy Beach (seated) and two music teachers established the "Beach Club" in Hillsborough, New Hampshire, to provide children with music education.

TIMELINE

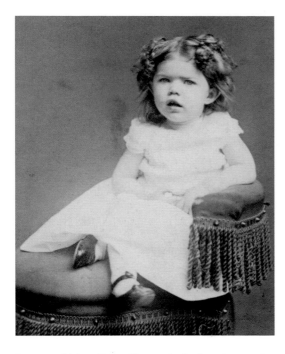

Two-year-old Amy Marcy Cheney sits for her photograph in Concord, New Hampshire.

1867 **September 5**—Amy Marcy Cheney born in West Henniker, New Hampshire, to Charles Abbott Cheney (1844–1895) and Clara Imogene (Marcy) Cheney (1845–1911).

1868 One-year-old Amy delivers "a perfectly correct alto to any soprano" that Mamma sings.

1870 At three, finishes reading her first book, *A Child's Dream of a Star* by Charles Dickens.

1871 Moves to Chelsea, Massachusetts; Amy permitted to play piano for the first time.
Summer—Without a piano, composes three waltzes.

1872 Amy Cheney is successfully tested for perfect pitch.

1873 At six, Amy begins piano lessons and general education under Mamma's instruction.

1875 Moves to Boston, Massachusetts, one of the leading musical communities in the nation.

1876 Johann Ernst Perabo, New England Conservatory piano instructor, replaces Mamma.

1878 **May**—Visits Aunt Franc (Emma Francis Marcy Clement) in San Francisco, California.

1879 At twelve, attends Whittemore's preparatory school in Boston; excels in all courses.

1880 **Fall**—Piano instructor Perabo and Amy visit poet Henry Wadsworth Longfellow; Amy plays piano for Longfellow and requests his signature for her autograph album.
December—Sets Longfellow's poem "The Rainy Day" to music as a gift for Aunt Franc.

1882 Professor Carl Baermann, former student of Franz Liszt, replaces piano instructor Perabo.

1883 Amy's song, "The Rainy Day" becomes her first published work.
October 24—At sixteen, makes debut in Boston Music Hall.

1885 **March**—Performs Chopin's Concerto in F Minor, op. 21, at the Music Hall with Conductor Wilhelm Gericke and the Boston Symphony Orchestra.
Arthur P. Schmidt publishes Amy's "With Violets," op. 1, no. 1. Over the next thirty years Schmidt publishes every composition she composes.
December 2—At eighteen, marries widowed surgeon Dr. Henry Harris Aubrey Beach.

1892 **February**—Mass in E-flat, op. 5, premieres at Boston Music Hall, performed by Boston's Handel and Haydn Society, conducted by Carl Zerrahn.

1893 **May**—*Festival Jubilate*, op. 17, premieres in Chicago, conducted by Theodore Thomas before an international audience; noted as the "success of the afternoon."

1894 Begins work on *Gaelic* Symphony in 1894.

1896 **October**—Boston Symphony Orchestra, conducted by Emil Paur, premieres historic *Gaelic* Symphony, op. 32.

1900 Beach performs her own Piano Concerto, op. 45 with the Boston Symphony Orchestra.

1905 **February**—Premieres her longest and most important solo piano work, *Variations on Balkan Themes*, op. 60, at a Boston recital.

1910 **June 28**—Henry Beach dies at age sixty-six.

1911 **September**—Sails to Europe; begins touring in 1912.

1914 **July**—Outbreak of World War I; she departs Germany early September for New York.

1915 **February**—Beach's *Panama* Hymn, op. 74, premieres on opening day of the Panama-Pacific International Exposition in San Francisco. In June, she attends Mrs. H. H. A. Beach Day in San Diego, California, to celebrate her music for the Panama-California Exposition.

1916 Over the next decade, Amy makes Hillsborough, New Hampshire, her official residence between concert tours.

1918 **February**—Performs concerts exclusively for Red Cross and other war relief until end of World War I; presents her music and that of Allied countries.

1928 **June 18**—Receives honorary master's degree from the University of New Hampshire, Durham.

1932 **April**—Visits First Lady Lou Henry Hoover at the White House.
June—Composes her only opera, *Cabildo*, op. 149.

1934 **April**—At the White House, the National League of American Pen Women celebrates the fiftieth anniversary of Beach's debut. Six months later, she is again honored for her Golden Jubilee by the Society of American Women Composers at the Chicago World's Fair.

1936 **April 17**—Beach and American Pen Women are White House guests of First Lady Eleanor Roosevelt; Beach performs *Three Piano Forte Pieces*, op. 128.

1940 **March 19**—Final performance at the Neighborhood Club in Brooklyn, New York.

1941 In frail health, composes last published work, *Though I Take the Wings of Morning*, op. 152.

1944 **December 27**—Amy Beach dies in New York, at age seventy-seven. She had directed her royalties be given after her death to the MacDowell Colony.

1999 Inducted into American Classical Music Hall of Fame and Museum in Cincinnati, Ohio.

MUSICAL GLOSSARY

anthem: A patriotic song, as in a national anthem; or a hymn sung by a chorus.

Chopin, Frédéric: (1810–1849) Born near Warsaw, Poland, Chopin was a self-taught virtuoso pianist and composer.

debut: To appear for the first time in public on stage.

flat and sharp: A flat (♭) in front of a note on a music sheet lowers the pitch by one half step; a sharp (#) raises the pitch by one half step.

harmony: Notes sounded simultaneously to produce chords; often in support of a melody.

key: The scale on which a music composition is determined; the key's name is based on the first note of the scale.

major key: A major key represents a composition that sounds bright or uplifting.

melody: A musical idea expressed in a series of musical notes.

minor key: A minor key represents a composition that sounds dark or foreboding.

Moscheles, Isaac Ignaz: (1794–1870) A Czech composer/piano virtuoso who settled in Leipzig (now in Germany).

musical prodigy: A young person who has extraordinary musical ability.

musicale: Typically, a small musical gathering or mini-concert in the privacy of a home.

opus: Latin for "work"; often used by composers to label and organize their published compositions; the first work is labeled as op. 1, the second work as op. 2.

perfect pitch: Rare ability to recognize the absolute sound (pitch) of any note heard, and identify it by key or letter name.

pitch: How high or low a musical note is.

score: A copy of music that a conductor uses that has parts for all instruments.

sonata: Instrumental music piece written for a soloist or a solo instrument with piano.

soprano: The highest singing voice.

staccato: Short, disconnected notes.

transpose: Using a different key to change music in a way that makes it sound higher or lower.

virtuoso: A performer with superb skills on his or her instrument.

waltz: A ballroom dance in three-quarter (¾) time; originally from Austria or Germany.

warble: To sing in a melodious manner with rapid changes between high and low.

SELECTED BIBLIOGRAPHY

All quotations used in the book can be found in the following sources marked with an asterisk (*).

Expert Consulted

Curtis, Liane, PhD, musicology. Founder and president of the Rebecca Clarke Society (rebeccaclarke.org) and the Women's Philharmonic Advocacy (wophil.org); author, educator, music critic. Interview by author November 16, 2018. Email correspondence November 2018 to May 2022.

Books

Ammer, Christine. *Unsung: A History of Women in American Music.* 2nd ed. Portland, OR: Amadeus Press, 2001.

*Block, Adrienne Fried. *Amy Beach, Passionate Victorian: The Life and Work of an American Composer, 1867–1944.* New York: Oxford University Press, 1998.

Elson, Louis C. *The History of American Music.* New York: Macmillan, 1904.

Jezic, Diane Peacock. *Women Composers: The Lost Tradition Found.* 2nd ed. New York: Feminist Press, 1988.

Neuls-Bates, Carol, ed. *Women in Music: An Anthology of Source Readings from the Middle Ages to the Present*. Boston: Northeastern University Press, 1996.

Pendle, Karin, ed. *Women and Music: A History*. 2nd ed. Bloomington, IN: Indiana University Press, 2001.

Tick, Judith. *American Women Composers before 1870*. Ann Arbor, MI: UMI Research Press, 2010.

Primary Sources

Beach, Amy. "How Mrs. Beach Did Her First Composing." *Musical America* 20 (August 8, 1914): 22.

*Beach, Amy. "Why I Chose My Profession: The Autobiography of a Woman Composer." Interview by Ednah Aiken. *Mother's Magazine* 11, (February 1914): 7–8.

*Cheney, Clara Imogene. [Biography of her daughter], signed February 26, 1892. Box 58. MacDowell Colony Papers, [pp. 1–13]. Manuscript Division, Library of Congress.

Henniker Historical Society and Museum, Henniker, NH. Correspondence. Amy Cheney Beach Collection. Box 14–1. Letter of October 27, 1941, Amy Beach to Marian T. Chase; Box 14–2, 14–3: handwritten notes, letters, newspaper clippings, articles.

Library of Congress, Manuscript Division. Marian MacDowell Papers; MacDowell Colony Papers. Manuscript Division, Box 1, Box 58.

Longfellow, Henry W. to Amy Cheney, November 15, 1880. Autograph Album, Folder 19, Box 1, Amy Cheney Beach (Mrs. H. H. A. Beach) Papers, 1835–1956, MC 51, Special Collections and Archives Division, University of New Hampshire Library, Durham, NH.

San Francisco Public Library, Bernard Osher Foundation Art and Music Center. Musicians' Letters.

Secondary Sources

Amybeach.org. "Amy Beach (1867–1944)." Go to: About> Timeline.

Block, Adrienne Fried. "How to Write an American Symphony: Amy Beach and the birth of 'Gaelic' Symphony." *American Composers Orchestra*, 1999.

Curtis, Liane, PhD, musicology. "Beach Breaks Through in 1892." *The Boston Musical Intelligencer*, November 10, 2017. classical-scene.com/2017/11/10/beach-1892.

_____. "Amy Beach at 150 Proclaimed." *The Boston Musical Intelligencer*, September 5, 2017. classical-scene.com/2017/09/05/amy-beach-150-proclaimed.

Hughes, Agnes Lockhart. "Mrs. H. H. A. Beach: America's Foremost Woman Composer." *The Simmons Magazine*, October 1911: 476–78. Periodicals Division, Library of Congress.

Library of Congress. "Biographies: Amy Beach (1867–1944)." loc.gov/item/ihas.200153246.

_____. "Recital by Mrs. Beach Arouses Wide Interest," *Evening Star* [Washington, DC], March 6, 1925: 17: chroniclingamerica.loc.gov/lccn/sn83045462/1925-03-06/ed-1/seq-17/.

Wilson, Arthur. "Mrs. H. H. A. Beach: A Conversation on Musical Conditions in America." *The Musician* XVII, no. 1 (January 1912).

Websites active at time of publication

TO LEARN MORE ABOUT AMY BEACH

At ten, Amy visited Aunt Franc in San Francisco, California.

Websites to Visit**

American Classical Music Hall of Fame. View Inductees: "Beach, Amy." Audio Tour. classicalwalkoffame.org/view-inductees/?id=9.

Amybeach.org. "Amy Beach (1867–1944): Celebrating a Great American Composer and Pianist!" Use the drop-down menu from the home page for links to a variety of Amy Beach's musical and life events. Go to: Music> Listen. Go to: About> Timeline.

Classics for Kids. Visit interactive links about composers, including Amy Beach. Listen to her *Gaelic* Symphony and music of other composers. Visit links: Explore More Composers; Women Composers of the Past; Listen to the Music; Compose Your Own Song; Instruments of the Orchestra; Musical Instruments; Different Instrument Families. Visit: classicsforkids.com; classicsforkids.com/show/?id=283; and classicsforkids.com/musical-instruments.

**Websites active at time of publication.

Places to Visit

New Hampshire

Henniker—Beach's birth home on Western Avenue (historical marker visible on fence; private home).

The Henniker Historical Society and Museum, 51 Maple Street.

Hillsborough—Beach's official summer residence for almost a decade; a piano presumed to be used by Beach resides at Fuller Public Library, 29 School Street, where Amy held Beach Club meetings for children.

Hillsborough Historical Society and Heritage Museum, 5 Central Street, houses a small exhibit on Amy Beach.

Boston, Massachusetts

The Boston Women's Heritage Trail. Beach's Boston residence at 28 Commonwealth Avenue is number two on the historical trail map. bwht.org/back-bay-east.

Historic 275-acre Forest Hills Cemetery, 95 Forest Hills Avenue, Jamaica Plain. Amy Beach's gravesite.

Edward A. Hatch Memorial Shell. Beach's name is displayed in five-inch bronze letters on the granite wall. She is the first female to join eighty-seven male composers.

Cincinnati, Ohio

American Classical Music Hall of Fame and Museum located at 1225 Elm Street. Step on pavement stones of inductees, including Beach's, at the Classical Music Walk of Fame.

ACKNOWLEDGMENTS

Many along the way helped breathe life into Amy Beach's story. With sincere appreciation to Liane Curtis, PhD, musicologist, whose expertise directed my research; for her generous time, meticulous review, and essential contributions; to Chris A. Trotman, Women's Philharmonic Advocacy's director of music publishing and editor-in-chief of the Amy Beach Project, for providing information vital to my initial groundwork.

Noted thanks for enormous aid in my research to Rebecca Chasse, photographic technician, and Bill Ross, professor and head, Special Collections and Archives Division, University of New Hampshire, Durham; Kristen MacLean, director, and staff, Henniker Historical Society; Colette Lucas, head librarian, and staff, at the MacDowell Colony; Loretta Deaver, reference librarian, Manuscript Division, and Arlene Balkansky, reference specialist, Library of Congress; Charles Shipman, supervisor, New Hampshire State Library, Concord; Christina Chadwick and Gary Sparks, co-curators, Hillsborough Historical Society and Heritage Museum; Stuart Hinds, curator of Special Collections and Archives, University of Missouri–Kansas City; Jason Gibbs, Art and Music Special Collections, San Francisco Public Library.

Special thanks to Jeri Chase Ferris, Kathy Wiechman, and Ginger Konvalin for steadfast support and pearls of wisdom; and to the Highlights Foundation for providing an educational, magical environment for this story to unfold.

With deepest gratitude to my editor, Carolyn P. Yoder, for her wealth of keen insight, vast contributions, and willingness to provide a professional forum. For her infinite patience and skillful guidance throughout my writing process; to Barbara Grzeslo, art director, for her remarkable gift of design.

Fond appreciation to Ryan, Eva, and Laura, for heartfelt enthusiasm along the way. Lastly, tender gratefulness to my husband, Tom, for his selfless, steadfast support to my writing endeavors; for willingness to lend an ear, and his gift of calm.

PICTURE CREDITS

Library of Congress: LC-DIG-npcc-25586: 33 (left).
University of New Hampshire, Mrs. H.H.A. Beach Papers, MC 51: 33 (right); 34; 38.

To my husband, Tom,
who believed in my vision,
and to my mother, Irene,
for her unwavering encouragement —CD

To Pee, thank you so much for your massive
support recently. And to Esmae, I hope you
keep going with your music lessons—
you have a great talent. —AJ

Text copyright © 2023 by Caitlin DeLems
Illustrations copyright 2023 © by Alison Jay
All rights reserved. Copying or digitizing this book for storage,
display, or distribution in any other medium is strictly prohibited.

For information about permission to reproduce selections from this book,
please contact permissions@astrapublishinghouse.com.

ISBN: 978-1-6626-8008-3 (hc)
ISBN: 978-1-6626-8009-0 (eBook)
Library of Congress Control Number: 2021925705

Calkins Creek
An imprint of Astra Books for Young Readers,
a division of Astra Publishing House
astrapublishinghouse.com
Printed in China

First edition
10 9 8 7 6 5 4 3 2 1

Design by Barbara Grzeslo
The text is set in Futura Medium.
The illustrations are done with Alkyd paint (a quick-drying oil paint)
with crackle varnish.